S0-ANF-350

AUG   1987

DUE DATE

DEC 01 1987			
	201-6503		Printed in USA

BARNARD NEW WOMEN
POETS•SERIES

HEREDITY

PATRICIA STORACE

BEACON ▾ PRESS ▾ BOSTON

Selections in this book have been previously published in *Sun and Moon, Arvon Prize Anthology 1980, Critical Quarterly, Michigan Quarterly Review, Paris Review, The New York Review of Books, Agni Review, Harper's, Secret Destination: Writers on Travel,* and *Parnassus.*

Grateful acknowledgment is made to the Corporation of Yaddo for enabling this book to be completed.

Beacon Press
25 Beacon Street
Boston, Massachusetts 02108

Beacon Press books are published under the auspices of the Unitarian Universalist Association of Congregations in North America.

92 91 90 89 88 87 8 7 6 5 4 3 2 1

Library of Congress Cataloging-in-Publication Data
Storace, Patricia
Heredity.
I. Title
PS3569.T648H4 1987 811'.54 86-47861
ISBN 0-8070-6800-4
ISBN 0-8070-6801-2 (pbk.)

for Louise Lovett,
Susan Ginsburg,
and in memory of Edith Zelnicker

▼▼

CONTENTS

▼▼▼▼▼▼▼▼▼▼
SOME LEGENDS

▼▼▼▼▼▼▼▼▼▼▼▼▼
SOME LANGUAGES

▼▼

INTRODUCTION

I don't know Patricia Storace, the poet, the person, the woman, so I can't introduce her to you. I have, however, read these poems many times over—first on request, asked to judge which of several arresting poets in the Barnard New Women Poets series might transit to a book of her own, and then for pleasure. So by way of introduction, I will describe the realm in which the pleasure of these poems lies.

Heredity is a courageous collection, even audacious. It's actually rather old-fashioned, involved very much with the past, yet strangely alive to the present, the senses, the erotic and the tactile. It's quite a daring combination, and it reminds me of two very different poets from the past. Listen:

"Pain is a master of protocol"
"When my breasts were no more than desire's fingerprints"
"Solitude makes a cathedral of the cell"
"I was fluent in you as in any French"

Can you hear the *sound* of John Donne and Emily Dickinson? I do. Not only rhythmically, which might depend on mere imitation, an ability to scan a line and recreate it, but in a manner less technical—the echo of these two poets in this poet's ingenuity, in her wit, in the truest and oldest sense of the word, in her intelligence. It is interesting to find in the late twentieth century a woman poet aiming at the startling surprise of the metaphysical style, the small shock, the mastery of an essentially classical fusion of form, tone, voice and meaning. I am entirely seduced.

"Seduced" means not only won over by the sound of the poet's voice, willing to listen to every syllable, given over to it, but also willing to wonder about the things she wonders about. There are no nuclear wars here, no affairs of state, no suicides or mad women. What there is is is the question the title points to—the question of heredity.

I see the "her" in "heredity" and note it as part of the landscape, not the whole ball game. As the poet spins her poems in blank verse or more rigid forms, she asks me to ask about what has been given in the past and what use or blight it might be in the present. This is Patricia Storace's theme—the question of legacy, genealogy, inheritance, the puzzle of descent. In the poems that most stay with me and in terms of the impact the entire collection has, this is a double concern: personal and cultural. I know nothing of the poet's personal history and cannot say whether two of the most stunning poems here—"Illegitimacy" and "The Archaeology of Divorce"—have anything to do with autobiography. It doesn't matter. Everyone has an autobiography; not everyone writes poems like these, their effect searing but oddly muted, held in check as poetry and not emotional orgy.

The second aspect of "heredity" is culture. What might the usable past be to the poet, to the reader, to any of us? This is a persistent intellectual theme throughout literary history, but it acquires a particular poignancy for women—shadowy figures in "The Great Tradition" of the literary past—and for an audience living in a period where everything seems created new for the moment and discarded, where historical ignorance is considered ordinary, and where history itself often seems relegated to last week's television newscast. Patricia Storace's poems stand against the tendency to forget or not to know where one has come from and what has come before. This is the "old fashioned" quality I mentioned earlier. It is literary. It toys with old forms like the villanelle, old figures like Eve, old periods like the antebellum South.

Why the poet examines the old, the past, the received is no mystery here. She tells us in "Varieties of Religious Experience:"

Myself, I tend to crouch and peer
in the classic posture of intent search,
bent, abject toward the missing object,

All this seems to me enormously original, as attitude and as poetic. The shades of Donne and Dickinson, themselves "in the classic posture of intent search" are smiling and join me in inviting perusal of what a talented poet has unearthed in her crouching and peering.

Louise Bernikow

▼▼▼

SOME LIVES

for my parents

SPRING AFTERNOON

The bank's tower without stained glass or chimes—
a grafting on the site of Saint Monica's church,
flashes for a changing congregation
news of warmer temperatures and passing time.

All of us grow taller by degrees,
shed defensive remnants of the winter's slouch,
and bodies, firm believers, prepare for private easters
with low-cut dresses, naked feet, bare knees.

The pavement, spendthrift, scatters fortunes of sun
and heat repaints the figures in the city's frieze
of lovers, thieves, and children still the right proportion
to find a shoulder broad enough to cry on.

I pass shops offering whips, spiked collars, devices
I don't need; to rack my neck requires
implements no sharper than a pair of lips,
and for bondage, simple genitalia suffice.

Some come to the docks for lovers,
but a few rebuffs, clearer than this swatch of Hudson,
indicate I leave my longing inland; that
my consent is to the river.

Still in my blonde decades of bright hair,
half-resigned to my legacy of absent Spaniard,
vanished Jew, true scion *ex nihilo*, I'm chafed
by the triple strand of Roman name I wear.

Descendant of nothing, a line too old to trace—
(*Debrett*'s finds us peerless)—no genealogist's
discovered who used first the dark devices of the eyes
or designed this particular heraldry of face.

3

These docks are grained with kin, no one's sons and daughters
living in a city where simple pilgrimage is possible
and a short walk conducts superfluous lives
into the presence of necessary waters.

Boat traffic constructs marine amphitheaters,
which crowd forward to spectators on the pier,
and the terraces of waves reaching their destinations
arrive as we will, tier shimmering on tier.

RUNNERS

for Darryl Pinckney

Listen: the key chains of the constellations are rattling the stars;
Morning's coming back, morning's coming home,
and fanned-out erstwhile landowners,
sleeping in flats like decks of cards
at the signal abandon their deepest dreams;
unraveling the ribbons of the present, they slide
onto terraces, draw blinds, and open the city's shutters
to survey its superterranean contours.
There's no land left; just ample deeds outside,
an outlook at most minimally rural
the stripes of green unbearable as yearning
and for some, afflicted with vertigo,
a prospect of panoramic suicide.
Still, dawn drives you down seven flights of stairs
each morning to attempt a fresh translation
of the homesteader's ancestral daylight craving
which, disinherited, you share,
to cover his land like the rising sun,
to ride out early through his fields
and wake each inch with a fertile eye.
Instead, you run;
the estate reborn beneath your feet is paved,
your muscles reclaim the concrete acres, fugitives
competing with the cars, that order of chrome celibates
who groan beneath day-glo habits, confessing
their futile wish to live.
Limbs broadcast with the seed of motion,
plowmen only of anatomy,
tending the last of inheritance,
your lungs and thighs your patrimony,
your body your plantation.

THE PUBLIC LIBRARY STAIRS

I.

Outside, everything is speaking at once—
a swamp steams with voices,
each creature set to its own tune,
in its own timbre singing the sentence of itself.
A shaggy-textured or smooth-shaven bark
tells what it knows of its tree.
Each fallen leaf with passion repeats
what it has learned of titi or swamp pine.
The tangled vines of the growing world
want witnesses, and clutch at us
to make us stay for one more minute of their story.

II.

Indoors, the world is motionless, and patient.
A mirror gives itself like a saint,
too humble to tell us who its parents are;
its answers translated into our tongue,
with inanimate honesty, tell us what we are.
In this cool hall, the marble floors endure us,
they carry our echoes faithfully,
those mysterious flora our feet plant here,
which will not take root, but open once and die.

III.

Businessmen in suits make a ladder of the stairs,
each step deliberate as a signature,
while old women make decisions at every step;
they hesitate, then standing on the precipice, drop
past couples, walking as steady as a heartbeat,
taking the stairs with a single strong sound,

even when the concrete brims suddenly with children,
foaming and flowing up and down,
plunging past like waters breaking from a dam.

A GIRL'S ROOM

for Felicity Rosslyn

Blue and white curtains, a French china plate,
whether summer months or winter dates,
coolness and quiet linger in this room,
the colors of permanent afternoon,
a climate the inhabitant admires,
at times achieves, more often just desires.
Claypots on bookshelves stand in an alcove,
as if plants were lyric, these books a grove;
both are set in sunlight, daily tended to,
the poets equal with the wandering Jew.

Houses confess to sour men and wives,
sterile rooms tell stories of bitter lives
and make unsuccessful hiding places,
as pots of rouge do for sallow faces.
We glimpse in proportions of instinct and art
the poverty-stricken or well-furnished heart.
When your windows open onto something new
where there's warmer shelter, a richer view,
may all that took root in your upstairs room
grow strong in your next house, flourish and bloom,
and complex passages sound natural and clear
from the chamber music you were writing here.

INTAGLIO

There are skills we need
no teaching to acquire.
At twelve, I discovered some,
when my breasts were no
more than desire's fingerprints,
smudges left on transparent glass
by someone distracted or called away
who'd be back in a minute
to drink it down.
My father decided
I needed shooting lessons
and hired a marksman
who earned his living
by giving exhibitions
of fancy shooting
at state fairs.
One Saturday, the marksman
and his dark-haired assistant,
who I realize now
must have been his mistress,
undertook my lessons
in a grove of pines
sweating turpentine
in the Alabama summer.
Adjusting my shoulder
to a twelve-gauge gun,
they warned I might
be startled by the noise,
"Say 'pull' when you're ready.
Relax. Now, have fun."
I only had to close my eyes,
release the catch;
five clay pigeons
disappeared, and on my cheek,
the scrape of marksman's beard

as a man gave me my first embrace
and said I was a natural.
We moved on, into close-range shooting,
with pistols, which need
more intimate targets,
in my case, a toy bear.
And as at short distance
I ripped its fur and
shot off its face
and flung it into air,
I noticed it hung
suspended between bullets
as if the air were
coiled with invisible rope,
with unseen nooses
that held it there.
As if death were a rainbow
arched from earth to sky.
God's pledge. Man's prayer.

VARIETIES OF RELIGIOUS EXPERIENCE

God wants us on our hands and knees.
So, at the right moment in the service,
we drop to the same level, hedges
pruned to equal height.
A woman near me settles into prayer—
a safe return to a well-lit house,
where nothing has been tampered with
and doors are firmly locked against intruders.
I envy her, this rose of prayer,
skirts rippling on the bench with faith,
carrying this Sunday's texts like dew,
neck curved less in submission
than in confidence, needing no more proof
than the unborn generations beneath her dress.
Her husband falls sharply to his knees beside her,
a soldier in a dugout, worshiping a different God
of deadly marksmanship, psalms riddling
his thoughts like snipers' bullets.
A few won't kneel, the diehard democrats
upright in their pews, polite but absolute
in the belief a man's as good as any king.
A grandfather mutters in the corner,
rocking in the cradle of his wish.
A housewife thumps down like dirty laundry
brought here for a scouring.
Myself, I tend to crouch and peer
in the classic posture of intent search,
bent, abject toward the missing object—
contact lens, wedding band, lost subway fare
the gritty pavement threatens to digest—
without which I cannot go home.

EXILE'S MATINS

Solitude makes a cathedral of the cell,
a dome of loneliness so vast
that every thought arrives a radiance,
an unexpected angel, starring the silence
with annunciations.
I have it both ways, as everybody does;
enclosure clasps me to the point of orgasm
at the same moment emptiness asserts itself.
I have no idea which to worship; I keep
two pillows on the bed, and wake,
body urgent to declare
real love for an imaginary wife.
I have the exile's faith; a kind of pantheism
inside out, a landscape multiple without a god,
promiscuous with absences
where bread leavens and wine ferments
negotiating only with decay.
The sinners disappear, but the sin remains,
stalking its forgiving.
The crucifix of waking I believe is real,
indomitable wood against a million spines,
the closest I can come to proof this dawn,
as the sun rises from its crouch
to make its expert incision in the night
gutting the darkness,
brandishing the black pelt whole.

AFTER PUSHKIN'S "WINTER EVENING"

Drink with me, old friend—
you held me like that when
I was a baby, thin-stemmed and precious
as that glass. Let's drink now
so we won't feel sad.
The carafe's half empty
and so are our hearts.
Sing me a song:
How the wounded falcon loved the czar's daughter.
Sing me a song:
And his beloved came to him, carrying water.

NOCTURNE

Nights are marine, and lavish with new darknesses,
not like years spent loving, territorial, which must be
circled by a ring, or sealed with the hyphen that
can be traversed in only two directions, narrow
track between last and first, or the monotonous reverse.
New tenants in each of our three former houses.
Fresh fatigue in rooms where we lay bedded,
our quilt, tree-of-life pattern, spilling on the floor;
the past crenelates and grafts a coral
of prefixes on the stem of verb we were.
Our own kisses splintered now, beneath the surfaces
of other loving, lie mineral; embedded.

ILLEGITIMACY

I.

An hour or two in bed—my family history.
I am caught in your act—like those cameras
planted in hotel rooms to catch
politicians at illicit sex,
I am the evidence of your kisses,
the proof of acts best unrecorded,
the reel of film replaying
the one domestic moment we three shared—
you begetting and begetting me.

Hence, the stigma of the illegitimate
in whom father and mother
are left coupling forever
so the child appears,
as it were, impaired,
conclusive proof of the social fear
that love outlasts lovers, and *is* eternal.
We bastards know it.
Trapped here in the love
that used a man and woman
as its instruments, it seems clear
that when the weather at last
turns radioactive,
and the temperature vaults
past boiling point
when the earth slips from the universe
like a hand from a black glove,
love will rush into the vacuum—
and caress it.

II.

Caught as I was in the spokes of your kissing,
I know the world as a web of unions
that words are the matings of syllables
that piano keys breed
as they lie beside each other,
that scissors are men and women;
two blades, they cut through anything
that obstructs their joining.

III.

Mother and Father,
lavish and careless
you left kisses everywhere
on the sheets on the glasses
on the walls on the night—
before you knew kisses were permanent.
One settled on my face,
and trembles there—
my mouth its imprint.

SUMMER TRINITY

I.

Sign of Cancer

The summer day recites an epic of its heat, twelve books
of rivulet and fire, of appetite's retreat into the body,
of cats pressed and lengthened by flatiron light,
of windows glazed with a sour mash of sun, 90 proof, mint July.
Across, the brick opponent of my address plays for a stake of air,
and drooling quadrants of window pane offer to the disciple street
their rusting mandalas of turning fans.
A parked car's front seat slumps on its wheel,
a leather image of a mortal crevice, accident
in which a body can slip forever.
Evangelical traffic lights are signaling the heat-lamed
crowds to cross, to walk, to change.
My own fan loosens dry sheaves of air,
which my lungs mill into days, nights, days,
into life which goes for now against the grain.

II.

Harvest

In the summer eyeball of the sky,
a rich blue glaze, heightened by capillaries
of tangled trees in this abundant month, child-bearing July
earth-making season of wheat and blueberry.

Oh summer. Summer. Now you fit my gaze
as a child's rump fits its mother's palm;
as lovemaking fits these heat-crowned days,
the living and to live attain their forms.

17

The sunset's a long kiss, and the table's laid
with porcelain on which a man, controlling the tremor of his wrist,
etched a brilliant pattern, adamantine brocade,
against his crackling fear of death, with which we dine,
we feast.

III.

August: Blues

Like a missing husband who keeps his keys
and shows up once a year,
August unlocks the back door,
slips upstairs and
climbs on top of her.

The fat air of summer, clotted with objects,
is overfurnished, like Victorian rooms
with antimacassars and ottomans,
a season imported from the colonies.
A woman sweltering inside stays.

Summer plans its coup, infiltrates by degrees;
clothes disband, heaped in corners like refugees,
while the crowbar of heat bludgeons
strangers down, and the sun wails
between their legs, and they wake where they fell,
next to each other, so thirsty.

RAINFALL

Because she is on the right side of the window,
it is an easy afternoon to love the rain,
because she does not hear what they are saying,
strain does not narrow in her sight the blessing
of those scarved and hooded walkers, dry as anti-wine,
beneath the inverse goblets of umbrellas.
Having spent the storm with him, her day makes simple,
harmless, this rainfall's cursive pencilings;
each life the child of beautiful plurals,
simple, simple, and beloved the world.

GRAND FINALE

Death does your makeup now,
and more precisely than you ever could,
applies its dark blue shadows,
irridescent, evenly around your eyes.

Monsieur death arranges your coiffure,
perfectionist. But after twenty sessions
of chemotherapy, unbeliever, you submit your hair
to the bridal wig and scarf of Jewish orthodoxy.

Fussy gourmand, death nibbles on your breasts;
he detests that fleshy butter spread
thick on skeletons, these bodies, fat-infested,
with their high, gamy reek, like venison.

Death, advanced technician, rewires your bones
to crack at the impact of embrace
amplifying, intolerably as microphones
the crescendo of loving from the not-so-quickly dying.

LA VALSE

He is dancing on the outskirts of her crinoline
restrained by satin walls.
Their speed lops off a corner dangerously
his partner nearly falls.
She is waltzing in the ramparts of her crinoline
on battlements of lace.
Her partner wolfs down chunks of air like meat
tormented by the pace.

And the layered phrases of the waltz
begin to lash his appetite
to plunge into the mille-feuille of her dress
and fill his empty glass and plate
with mouthfuls of rich love, vintages of death.

They are circling in the vortex of her crinoline
swept down the mirrored halls.
The whirlpool of her skirt sucks fire from
the sconces on the walls.
And the pastry catches flame
and the bottles of champagne
explode, and the planet of the room
the man and woman disappear.

A Pause; and then the music starts again,
the ladies link hands with the men,
and the violins tucked under chins
unbolt the bars of music and begin
and the helpless partners hurtle on
while the spectators applaud
the risk that makes the sport so good,
the chance that love with a ballistic force
might throw the missile-couple off its course
while the fuselage of music melts
and the two careen past tenderness

beyond the gravity of hate
flash past the blur of other lives
and neither one survives
neither one survives.

STILL LIFE

Somehow, the two of us sit in a café
bordering the park. Its grass succumbs
again to chronic green, and I see,
obedient, what I don't want to see—
lacerating tulips, leaf-racked trees,
hear steps as gunshots on the street,
heel and pavement sniping at each other.
The corner of your mouth bleeds geography
in the form of Côtes du Rhône.
And the sunset is cossack,
reddening the West with its pogrom.
I should be sipping the Riesling of an April evening,
the minutes sweet and disappearing on my palate,
mouth smoothing out, from time to time,
the folds of your neck's mortal velvet.
I should admire, not endure, the hyacinth, the campanelle
developing their color photographs of light.
But an hour not this one has stiffened
on the clock, and will not pass;
and eternity, twelve-armed goddess
revealed to me, appears in her aspect of hell.

RECLUSE

I have gouged out the eyes of my house.
My windows are double-thick and smoked.
Light attempts their steely mist, but falls down dazed,
lame; a bird crippled by its own reflection,
struck down at introduction to its own glazed self.
Still my body insists on night and day
and will be exercised, like some demanding pet,
the thoughtless gift of some misguided neighbor.
The living cannot colonize the floor of sleep,
divers who lack the right equipment
and come gasping up for consciousness,
lungs ravenous.
Seeing this, I am agnostic toward my death
which may turn out to be a wakeful twilight,
nothing so desirable as eternal rest.
For years I have refused all visitors
but uselessly, as absence grows more dense
and populated, hotel without a single vacancy.
I entertain like a politician's wife,
helpless hostess to unwanted guests,
chatting with the shifting nameless in the room,
seeing to the comfort of the well remembered.
Old virgin, I have shared my bed
with more men than a whore.
Recently, I have stopped the groceries,
the weekly cartons of cereal and eggs,
but the mind makes its breakfast
polishing its plate of wit's leftovers.
I have done all I can,
making sure that nothing will be delivered.
Not milk. Magazines. Myself.

TWO HATS: A FANTASIA

The worlds collect under two summer hats
adjacent on a terrace on an island.
Late sun aligns a wheat-hued Panama
with a green straw, broad-brimmed, abundant,
wheel-rimmed and still beneath the burning magnet.

Hurl the green straw to heaven like a comet,
I shall take her upstairs and kiss her in a hammock,
wind-driven kisses, deciduous, uncountable,
gilding her breasts with the gold leaf of my tongue,
Sunday-ravished Christian, speaking in tongues—
I'll take that Panama between my teeth,
deposed regime dropping from my balcony,
and hold him as font bathes christening child,
and teach him how to cultivate the dusk,
gardening the shadows' topiary, the two of us
will decant the dark, savor night's bitter chocolate.

Two hats on reed matting near a numbered key,
the door open to the balcony providing a brilliant
partial view of such dunes, such deltas, such indentations
and revisions, a coastline glistening, altering,
within the fluent narrations of the sea.

A WEEKEND AT THE LAST RESORT

Pain is a master of protocol.
No matter how established an acquaintance,
one descends in formal dress,
marveling at the nicety of arrangement
the jewelry of attentiveness to guest,
a finesse of patterning noose to neck,
or coil of woman gripping child,
the narrow gap in the balustrade
measuring the man who fell.
Here, a kiss of welcome tightens
on the temples like electrodes,
and a man's eye, assessing
from a distance a certain woman's
breast, leaves noticeable welts.
Lighting here is such that mirrors
report depth as well as outline,
hair is registered by follicle,
metal gleams inside a tooth's enamel,
and along with hip and abdomen,
underlying entrails pried to sight.
If we love in darkness, we suffer in detail.
Barefoot on this walled estate,
there's a cusp of glass indented to each arch.
Beneath a constellation's cutting edge,
a shard of star is fitted to each eye.
In the library hangs the celebrated canvas
of three plums clustered on neutral satin,
which prove, on moderate scrutiny,
to be drops of blood, emerging
on the moiré whorls of fingertip.
Guests pause here before dinner,
like their predecessors; some wonder
what might change, if love were furnished
with comparable craftsmanship,
or took such pains.

THE ARCHAEOLOGY
OF DIVORCE

We examine today not sacked cities, but sacked lives.
We have studied destruction on a larger scale.
Now we turn to the war between female and male,
the wounds delivered by husbands and wives.

Sir: You really think these failures are related?
Yes, Klein, I have seen impregnable city walls
brought down by convulsions in trivial halls
and cannot think my ideas outdated.

We proceed to the objects salvaged from downstairs.
Shards of the bedroom have their strong appeal,
I admit, but what we find here may help reveal
another aspect of this savage pair.

We assume the couple used to dine in this space.
I emphasize a fact undergraduates may miss—
the same mouths share bread as vulnerably as kiss;
that board, like their bed, brought them face to face.

Here is the table; note these fine archaic knives.
The flesh we scraped from one might indicate
a practice occurring even at this date:
perhaps the two ate each other alive.

At any rate, a struggle: the outcome isn't known.
Look, the chairs overturned in terrible haste,
the bowl of fruit left to rot and waste,
and this carcass of love, gnawed to the bone.

CHANSON DE MAL-MARIÉE
(13TH CENTURY)

His first task; to kick me with his heavy boots,
then pinches, slaps, and if not too drunk,
the bastard pulls my hair out by the roots.
He doesn't give gold; just black and blue—
brute!

His sole occupation is taunts and clouts,
our rent consists of my tears and pleas,
but if dinner's meatless, his highness pouts,
and smashes plates like my girlhood dreams—
lout:

A stronger man once helped me from the street,
and bought me salve to heal what you had bruised.
Don't snigger; we might find a way to meet,
invent less violent uses for our hands,
sweet . . .

I'd cook him wild mushrooms, a chicken, stewed,
the tender amber of an apple tart,
and after chilled white wine and savory food,
we'll lie down for an after-dinner nap—
nude.

AFTER A CHORUS FROM
THE BACCHAE

Like a torrent of waters, I fall to my God,
like a woman ready for a child,
I come for him, the father of my child,
the world is too small for what I need;
the God can give it.

I drove like an ax through the forests
swift as famine through hot fields of grain
the cliffs snatched me in their beaks,
who is he, the father of my child?
Let him know this song.

She is perfect, the woman
the God touches, teaching her to yearn.
She is his corn, and he scatters her
She is his wine and he drinks her down
She is his shore and he meets her
She is his lioness who brings him meat,
the air in the lungs of the breathing God.

DEATH: A BETROTHAL

This long engagement makes me restless.
At first, unhappy with the arrangement,
I rebelled.
To my parents, eager for the match,
I said we had nothing in common.
You were a catch, my mother promised,
that girls in every state would envy.
My father said you were the last tycoon,
whose millions drowned his little salary.
You swore that I would want for nothing
when we married; kissing my hands,
you left these slashes on my wrists,
the marks of your affection.
The scar on my forehead is your signature,
stating in your bold script,
"I don't forget you, though I seem far away."
The suspense between my heartbeats is your serenade,
the soundless moment in the ceremony
when bride and groom exchange their rings,
the pledge that says you will come back for me.
I am quilted in your courtship—
whipping around hairpin curves,
I feel the extent of your embrace.
You scatter the highway with valentines,
birds with sheared-off wings,
bloody baubles of dog and deer.
I trust you, though my mother says
no man cleaves just one woman.
I train myself to be a perfect wife.
When creatures telegraph themselves
from right to left
across the freeway, left to right,
I intercept their messages for your sake.
Speeding toward my wedding day,
I never swerve. I don't brake.

WINTER BREAKFAST

Strange, how with one night's exception,
I associate you with the morning;
alchemist of the coffee pot, humming
and measuring the coffee shavings
into a wizard's hat of paper filter,
extracting our drink of hot black velvet.
As I remember—I'm squeezing oranges—
and your dark skin, the petulant mouth,
the vital daylight sparkle of your eye,
the night-formed new crystals of your beard,
return, thick with seed and shred,
fibrous and essential as the juice I'm crushing
from that fruit, as my self, long lost and perpetual.
This is painful. But the old plenitude wounds more
sharply than the present loss I know as natural.
When I think of how your features looked in the lake
of mine, how your eyes and mouth still waver there,
vanishing and clear, I'd like to cry.
On Sundays, I'd make bagels I taught
myself to make, adding salt, a tablespoon of malt,
to the gluey dough we boiled and baked.
You'd bite the muscular crust of the ring,
with your strong teeth, eating through to the central nothing.
I'd like to cry. At the same time I rarely wonder
where you're living now, and never imagine the interior.
Strange to have arrived at a blithe curiosity, marvelously mild,
which I recognize as pain's wife, the photograph
ready in his wallet to show strangers discreetly
puzzling what she looks like, who on earth could love him.
Well. For us, new snapshots on the desk,
the telephone's dead. The light bills are paid,
and after seven years, we've renewed our cells.

BLIZZARD

Crossing the sheerest borders of the sky, the emi-
        grating
silent populations of the snow arrive
to find a reception concrete if unwelcoming.

A storm of Parthenon might look like this, drifting toward
        Piraeus,
when architects with other purposes than building
graft the atoms of their marble with motions it protests.

Here in the human melting pot, tears only cousin these crystal
        dissolutions
falling to nothing or to no avail, somewhere,
always, with monumental liquid persistence.

SIMPLE SUMS

Midnight; supernatural shadows on the kitchen tiles.
No clever housewifery eradicates these stains.
When human light retires, reappears upstairs,
darkness alone solves the problem of this room,
shifts chairs where they should be, thrusts table against door,
settles to a night of gambling,
rolling, retrieving its black dice on the floor.

A mouse inches forward, circles a cheese shard—
like an errant ace cut back into its deck,
his body's dealt forever to a flat steel card.

The arithmetic of love or pain is so exact.
Think of a woman's womb; its nine-month estimate,
rounding off a percentage of desire.
One animal tonight miscalculates
and writhes out a correction of its error.
Exemplary scholar, its neck snaps—
describing precisely the structure of its trap.

BEDTIME PRAYERS

How in this world of wicker and stuffed bears
did it happen? This bitter girl and burning boy
beneath the pink gingham and Black Watch plaid,
a traitor pair, resist the nightmare monarchy of Mom and Dad.

So little sweetness in this rose-papered room
where infants wriggled on the nipple's hook
and learned self-hatred from their mother's look,
and her traditional admonishment, "Go to your womb."
And now I lay me down perverse,
crushed under masonry of father's curse.

Tonight, lovers leaping to each other's arms
across the precipice of past,
as limbs merge in erotic galaxies
now, as the Olympic blood wheels fast
runs with red gospels through the arteries,
can parent-current and tide of child converge,
and God make us ardent, and merciful,
for what we are about to conceive?

STORYBOOK ENDING

The book's too valuable for her, an antique
heirloom, printed in Edinburgh on Paternoster Row,
one hundred and twenty-five years ago. Her father's mother's siblings
signatures possess it one by one with copperplate flourishes
of street and state; terse male, baroque female names, neuter dates,
like skaters' school figures on frozen lakes loop and
mate opposite the frontispiece, under the title, *Stories of the Greeks*.
She's told not to play with it too often, but daily can't resist
immersion in engravings of Paris and Oenone, or Odysseus
and Penelope, for whom she's named her Ken and Barbie,
the man and woman healing mouth to mouth on the last
page of the Odyssey. When the book's bedded in its slipcase,
it's a private ecstasy to finger the gilt-edged pages,
smooth, cool, and justified perfectly as piano keys.
In summer, when it was still light at eleven,
the season taught her the new skill of lengthening
her living in the stories. Her mother comes in thin negligee
for prayers; to close curtains and shut the door.
Downstairs, she hears her father's key; he's late
as summer nightfall; a thin Niagara sounds; of bathwater
her mother's drawing, one bare knee touching the cold tile floor.
It's safe now to slip the book back into bed,
the blue and gold volume on her flat chest luminous
and intimate, a moon guiding a tide of dreams, none
tonight of burning cities, treachery, or dying friends.
No. She's grown into a goddess, all floral curve of breast and thigh,
going naked as the pictures show immortals do, embraced
by a hero, dreaming of her divinity, she sleeps
under ancient sentences, a child the book is changing
into someone human.

AFTERNOON ABSTRACT

One late afternoon, when the light has had a stroke,
and the poorly circulating sky's gone gray,
and you've been having a picnic with your life,
and pack up the basket, recork the inch of wine,
before a storm dismembers the pretty day,

your life tilts your head back to face the clouds
and compares them to heroic abstract paintings,
the perfect, dying, accidental convolutions
whole shapes and colors drifting off forever,
the Pollock paintings, which each time you look, you never see again.

Taller, stronger, hungrier than you, he takes you home,
chattering incessantly, willful and unfaithful as a husband.
You fill a plate for him, and when he's done, cradle
your life's heavy head between your breasts; then,
beyond bravado, you beg him not to leave you like a man.

SOME LEGENDS

for the Wyatt family

PERDITA

The world is thick with women.
How will I tell whose midnight dream I am
when houses beat with them, and every bed
has held its cluster like a night-ripe vine?
The trees keep watch with their women's eyes,
there may be granite made of women—
she may not be a woman now.

She clings to me like water.
A sea of her moves with me when I move;
transparent as God, too intimate to know,
she keeps my breathing like a secret.
My words run naked toward her.
Like animals, I know them by her mark.

Oh, mother, I am born.
I have taken your throat, your stranger hands.
Did you notice when I won them in our wordless chess?
See, the breasts have kindled on my body like stars
whose light has taken years to reach the earth.
My muscles have drunk all your shadow.
My own eyes have claimed all your tears.

BARBIE DOLL

I.

Her body, which is perfect,
is impenetrable.
It is her capsule,
orbiting
through childhoods which follow
childhoods which follow
childhoods,
the nest of decades
that emerge from one another.
Children are her oxygen.
The life oils in their hands
have made her plastic
tougher than muscle or bone.
The one way to destroy her
is dismemberment.
Her perfection is a violence.
Fling her to the soil;
she stands upright and
quivers, a thrown knife.
Grasp her carelessly,
her feet and hands
can damage, the flesh
laddered suddenly with blood.
One of the small things
that cause consequences;
a slap, a razor,
a pinch of cyanide.
One of the things
whose smallness is a honing;
a piranha,
the switchblade of the ocean.

II.

The waist is rigid as a doctrine,
the body formed to carry clothes,
the feet shaped to stiletto heels,
frozen into point, the toes.

Marked with factory signature,
yields to credit or to cash,
made not to caress, but pose;
modeled for a camera flash.

The fingers durable and plastic
webbed together, form a hand,
the third emerges like a thorn,
soliciting a wedding band.

The detail royal on all the gowns
pearls sugaring the wedding dress,
a perfect doll, unbreakable;
stony and nippleless, the breasts.

ITHACA

I.

Scavenger, a harp string pecks in the banquet hall.
Flung on the floor in strips, the late sun, flayed.
A restless queen waits for guests and servant girls
to cull an alcove's sanctuary, lie down dark. To prey.

Upstairs, an oily flame aspires to a spine,
evolving shadow vertebrae; object and body bargain
to exchange conditions; a chair, hard carved pine
and scholar, outlines and comments on the queen's position.

Now Penelope lifts the iron of the day, sets sail
above the pooling lyric gossip of the local bard.
Textiles spraying at her feet, scrolls of colored wools
make Ithaca quiver; shores course toward their lord.

She thinks: the bed's a gulf where exiled men and women wander
in darkness, sometimes in each other's arms recur,
feel lost kisses in the currents of their hair, like sediment, still stir.

A year away, Odysseus sews home, tracing the pattern of the land,
threading nine years' silk through a phosphorescent eye;
the thick wake ribbons from the needle of his craft, and terns
open-winged on straits of air, figure flights of outstretched hands.

II.

Keep your distance, stranger.
Stand closer to the fire
whose light makes
unknown bodies legible
where mobile flame
and unexpected shade
complete a continuous

narrative of feature.
Cold scrutiny of heat
preserved these halls.
As winter tests landscape
and all its claims to life,
I test your claim
that we are man and wife,
whether you are husband
or impostor-suitor,
some blood-stained harlequin,
composite of them all.
Stand closer to the fire.
The source of my fidelity
was not blind observation
of some abstract law,
no: honed precision of desire.

OLD TESTAMENT GOD

Are you still there?

Were you the corrupt girl who drove the nail
through the forehead of the evil general?

Did you hate the inattention of men drinking, women laughing?
Did you destroy the exquisite golden calf?

Are you there, old Caretaker, Heartbreaker, Supreme Plague-
Maker, old Festival of miracle and massacre,

blood-ambitious knife in the father's absolute hand,
nomad impulse lusting to be kinged, immutable, Divine Command?

When praised, were you vicious, did you spurn your psalmist?
O most exalted, then you do exist.

FIRST LOVE

When you are tuning my body with your eyes,
it seems the dead wouldn't need bodies
to stay alive, it's a strange surprise
that anyone living will ever die,
and all the words for our hopes of peace,
of love, of truth, are wordlessly the color of your eyes,
changing like seasons in the light of mine.
When I move to the chorus of your looking
I'd be a fool not to know I've lived
forever in these days with your glance
engaged to mine, and my eyes becoming apples
ripening, perfectly attached to the branch of your gaze.

EVE'S KNOWLEDGE

I remember a fiery angel at the gate
driving us into a book called Genesis.
My nipples will not again point due north,
drawn by the true magnets of your palms,
and Gihon, Pishon, Tigris, and Euphrates
are only caesuras, moistening Eden's lost quatrain.
Dear Adam, we are sentenced; our bed's made
not with damask, but with sheets of paper.
Within severe margins, we're granted perfect binding.
Like a lucky couple, we've slipped off
to lie down together in a silent forest.
Our act of union's here, between chastened pages
of guardian evergreens that have come to us
to teach us love according to the letter.
Where there are no seeds, there are no predators.
Now you and I know such white bravery of nakedness
that neither will blush or grope for clothes
or need here the sometime mercies of the rains
or hope for the tender cowardice of shade,
though the print of your molars on my left
shoulder, your real flesh, sealed, and
scripture of your sweat again against mine,
would, God knows, be infinitely better.

GENESIS

I think it isn't true, the tag *nihil ex nihilo*,
as love gestates in void,
as the round emptiness of that salt-glaze vase
is the initial gesture of embrace,
and lilac inclines to it,
filling it with flowering.

And loss is oxygen to love
as the various widowed learn,
loving without hope; but no one lives
without imagining a love, yearning
to repatriate a dear, lost body in his arms.

And love is pressed molten from the voices of the wronged,
love erupts like magma from our deaths—
torch song.

FORTIES MOVIE, STARRING JOAN CRAWFORD

When she wakes, spread on terraces of pillows,
hungover in sheets with alençon edges,
she thinks, I am . . . I dreamed . . . a melon
out of season, in the window of a fancy store,
and last night, that broad-shouldered doctor I met
bought me; he divided me into wedges.

I don't dream of my husband; I sleep with him,
when he's not shacked up with his girl, that toilet,
with her double-bed ass, and her three fat brats
she keeps in sneakers and denim, that sloven,
she didn't have the brains to saddle cash,
    that factory discount courtesan.
I'm sure that's the word, if that's how you pronounce it.

God, I hate to remember that scene in the nightclub
when I said I was pregnant, so he married me,
our wishes were granted; it's been a Grimm's story.
I could use a martini, even if it's too early
and the damned maid's a snoop. Christmas is coming
and I'll be the tree, hung with rubies,
an earring to celebrate each ovary,

and it's time for a car, and a couple of dresses,
a chiffon one, maybe, angelic and flowing,
a sweet little costume for the savior's day.
I'd better lose weight, or I'll look like my mansion,
and yes, I'm due for some dyeing again,
these rinses don't last, my goddamned roots are showing.

48

KING LEAR BEWILDERED

The leaves are storm-rattled jester's bells
and the king without a court goes courting—
glass chips, lead slivers, seeds in a gourd,
a churning debris in his jester pulse.

And the lacerating gale, tough-thrashing, is leather
on flesh, as he looks for his girls,
trampling the spongy, pubic heather.

Oh my body, girl-child, lashed here this ugly night,
shall I lead you out of rain, little one shall I carry you,
I'll dry your soft hair, daughter, the strange snow
drifting on my chest, knotted, now so weirdly white.

When the mushroom rose between my legs,
I fungus-fathered three, three
fertile daughters. Not one of them can bear me.

SWEET HOME

They sat, cross-legged child Yogis,
formal and upright before the TV,
but felt that they were lying on their backs,
beneath the machine's changing cloud pictures,
motorboats, saloons, weather maps crayoned
with frowning and smiling suns,
like masks of mass tragedy and comedy.
The dinner bell rings, chilly and superior,
in the arctic tones of someone who won't play,
threatening the ones who do, who dawdle on their way
to fried chicken, ice water, and frozen peas.
"Salt and pepper please and what did you do today?"
When they tell, Dad says "Impossible" and "Rigmarole,"
meaning some harm, some good, but nothing
of the kind that is coming to them all.
One child frays a cuticle until it bleeds
a red holly berry on the paper napkin.
Mother says "Don't" and "Stop" and once, "God damn it."
Her eyes are red as traffic lights.
She doesn't eat her hot fudge sundae,
and leaves the table, though they all see
her eyes are shining like the pruning shears
ordered in December that came yesterday.
The children eat their ice cream anyway.

SOUTHERN HOSPITALITY

Two feet, matched white plumes, rest
on the jewel case velvet of a footstool;
like the decor, dress, and ice cream you preferred,
your desserts and furnishings were rose-colored.
While the downtown stores held moving sales,
reincarnating in suburbs with utopian names,
you in your inner city (six stories of
apartments for the genteel old),
served trays of chicken salad beneath the ceiling fan,
cleared, and winking, "Everything must go,"
set down two scoops of peppermint for each,
in Empress Eugenie's pink cut-glass bowls.
The ice cream melted like the afternoon,
like ideologies and cotton wealth,
and you told stories of your gray-eyed mother,
a German Jew who crossed in fifty-eight,
emigrating from pogroms to the War Between the States.
Sixteen and alone, red braids intricate around her head,
eventually the vowels of the Yiddish prayers she spoke
slept in a Southern accent like a featherbed.

ANTEBELLUM ARCHITECTURE

I.

Wrong Side of the Tracks

Sunday and the sun of it white like spilled flour
sifts through the mesh Seurat of a screen door,
pointilliste on plastic foliage, bright handful of
        buckshot on the linoleum floor.

Inside and outside finally share one bed together, share a name,
hot illicit union unconcealed, sealed, ordained
with savage services by a born-
        again September hurricane.

A dirt road runs red past a creek, brown lukewarm coffee,
where Mama totes endearments to trade for groceries,
Mama's so smart, she knows how to float on the sucking
        quicksand of courtesies.

Papa paws with one hand through his favorite Sunday funnies,
with the other the breast of his sixteen-year-old Tommye,
who sits on his lap for a slip and barrette she'll get
        if she's real sweet to Daddy.

O Precious Lord. . .temptation. . .sinners. . .moans a neighbor's radio
and then through the syrupy harmonies, an alto solo
whiplash rips at God, and Papa yells, "can't a man get peace—
        turn off that trash!"

II.

Right Side of the Tracks

On the tall easel of a sumptuous, shaded hill
rests the spotless canvas of an ivory house
where generations paint self-portraits, self-flattering, detailed.
There's Mama in the shape of a silver epergne

hung with crystal baskets for fruit and sweets,
quite valuable now though once thought vulgar
when Papa acquired her after the war.
A black maid, white-uniformed, painted in a corner,
polishes her, preserving the balance of the color scheme.
Look! Grandfather rendered as Confederate banknote,
and Grandmama above him on a pedestal,
a miniature bottle of smelling salts.
A half-drunk glass of bourbon, recognizable as Brother Keene,
and Aunt Violet, before the breakdown, hot and hysterical
gibberish flaming beneath the decorous Victorian mantel,
all visible through the spaces of six white column daughters,
spinster, architectural, bearing classical caryatid names,
the six perfect penises of Papa's secret dreams
starched petticoats stiffened into plaster
draped with sweet garlands of Papa's pleading,
"Don't leave me Corinna, Camilla, Virginia,
keep house for me Doric Ionic Corinthian my daughters,
so lightly laden with my history my daughters stand
still, keep house, keep my house standing."

DEEP SOUTH CAROL

Dry county, where afternoons, sprawled on their backs,
the housewives reel from Southern air, viscous as cognac,

and the saved on Baptist steps, in Greek revival hairdos,
letter the Sunday text, "What do Jesus think of you?"

And the one grand house is empty; its peeling columns stand
like discarded muskets, emptied of ammunition.

Everything's costumed; hoopskirted rustling oak trees
furred with Spanish moss, whisper at factitious pedigrees.

The scattered lakes glint hot and jagged as trash tin,
and slaughtered Indians sun there, reborn as water moccasins.

The squatter woods are full of decomposing cars,
and menopausal, yellowed, hag refrigerators.

A screen-door cooks unhinged in the sun;
a tubercular mattress dies at length, coughing cotton.

Jesus serves passing cars at a gasoline pump.
The Holy Family farms near the city dump.

Black and shirtless, he walks home in beltless jeans,
a swan of shadow swimming after him,

avoiding that charged tree where his father died.
O little town of Bethlehem, how you still lie.

THE SHERIFF IN THE WESTERNS

The country itself is what keeps the peace.
The sheriff is its tree, where bad men hang.
Now he's the track that casts in clay
the robber's accidental footprint, now
the branches crackling underfoot,
the stones that make the horses lame.
He is the hailstorm forcing them to camp.
The sheriff follows himself where he leads
and ends at the hideout of the whole gang.

He takes his orders from the sun itself.
Together they pour on the heat and parch
the thieves until their tongues are black.
The sheriff and his posse ride for hours,
"Not a trace of anything," the deputy complains.
The sheriff shrugs and points to buzzards overhead.
A white flag inches like a rattler from a cave,
but the sheriff knows how to handle snakes,
he holds his gun ready, fingering the catch.

The sheriff breaks up brawls in the saloon,
a single kick divides the double doors,
each half a tablet inscribed with commands.
He smashes the bottles of molten gold
that make the ranchers imagine they are kings.
Through him, the land renders them its blows,
they remember the miles that walloped them like slaps,
the brain concussions of so much empty space.

The outlaws in the jail are threatening the sheriff,
taunting him, rattling the bars of their cells;
he peers between the bars, to oil-veined acres,
he listens to the words that promise dollars,
he looks into their eyes, they show him death.
The sheriff takes his coffee and a book,

and sits down in his armchair on the porch,
he rocks beneath the broad-shouldered sky,
his lips move a little as he learns to spell.

Pressed against the territory of his chest,
his star attacks the dusk with violent light
a gate through which no stranger bullets pierce,
that dams the angry trespass of his blood,
it glitters intensely as the evening star
that mounts its guard between two worlds,
and mediates between the hostile pair,
prevents the earth's exploding into heaven,
and staves off from above the black ambush of night.

NATIVITY SCENE

Confined fire in its stone pit, the blazing elemental child
toys with its mother's burning ruby jewelry,
with rings, beads, bracelets, coronets of flame;
Near the warmth on a bed of straw,
with her fresh-born son, lay Mary.
Tonight carnivorous winter winds are gentled,
the cannibal earth is sheltering
and death is a guest unwelcome but familial
in rooms of danger made habitable
washed with water drawn from arctic grieving,
clear now, warm enough for bathing.
An arrow centered at its soft target, the baby
feeds from the nipple's natural charity,
drinking milk from the holy human breast,
while she strokes his first natural crucifix of spine,
and leans like a ship on its passage home
against the North Star of Joseph's chest,
and knows this embracing is nativity.
The world was always pregnant with the child,
but cradled by her lover, cradling their son,
incarnate god, incarnate man and woman,
this was the birth of the virgin, Mary.

PAMINA'S MARRIAGE SPEECH

We thank you all for your congratulations,
for the staves you loaned us
to lean on through the trials.
I hope I won't darken our celebrations
if I affirm my marital consent
with an honest, but agnostic epithalamion,
in praise of that dubiety, sustained connection,
and love, that questionable reality,
unlikely, but possible, like resurrection.
I say this as I place a husband's hand
beneath the breast so intimate
in act two with a knife,
exchanging steely certainty of blade
for malleable gold of wedding band.
Guard, oh my husband of the literal sex
against the male bias toward the radiant spasm
of heroic loss, sad captains gathered
at the last feast to applaud
the old lion's shaggy, final roar
and toss love on the fire, ecstatic holocaust
suspiciously similar to male orgasm.
You see the carnal parallel I make;
so I too, for my husband's sake
will discipline my woman's love
of endless possibility, the maenad's
blind absorption in sensation,
the response, naïve, momentous,
to any cynic's predatory kiss
by which our love of fresh beginning, generation,
follows bad directions and misprinted signs
to that much-used freeway, promiscuity.
Remember, too, that love contains, but is not an emotion;
is not romance, that color photograph
of a smiling couple on a short vacation
whose kisses are purchased, pretty souvenirs,

in gabled shops with good views of the ocean.
Love is, in supreme form, concentration.
Enough of this. Raise the veil, beloved,
now I've made it dark enough to kiss
and teach those guests we've rendered skeptical
love passionate as doubt, as radical.
By these hands' imperfect light
receive a resonance of knowledge,
through flickering palms, lucid embrace,
read by this uncertain flame,
achieve description of a face.
Pray that we withstand the shock of blessing,
assembled friends, with lowered heads,
pray urgently that we may make
for good the crucial and ecstatic risk
we take, following brilliant torches to this bed.

▼▼

SOME LANGUAGES

for Igor Gerashchenko and
Irina Ratushinskaya

VERSE, REVERSE

Such eros in the early, oral roses,
such blush and spread, such floral pregnancies;
the trees elaborate comprehensions of the sun
in green nuances and leafy, lush vocabularies.
New wheat of words proliferates in throatfuls
and nothing is mistaken.
There's spring in thinking and its thrust and cling
reverse and turn to its beginnings in the body's fluencies,
where we've read the elegant English of an eye,
known the anguished Russian recited in the groin,
fingered the underlying elegies in bone:
it's there; first in the structure of torso and hip,
it's there where lip rhymes couplet with lip
and hand translates a breast so delicately,
and tongue interprets tongue with such fidelity
that all the eras sweeten in the early, oral roses.

SONG OF SALT AND PEPPER

Dinner twins,
who remind us that nothing
we know of remains uncoupled or
unparalleled, you revolve from hand to hand,
place to place, like seasons circling
each other in different hemispheres,
converging and married on our evening plates.
One of you, the center of the sea and tears,
reminds us that there is no food
we eat without a bitterness,
that pleasure stings and is
endured like pain;
your mate burns our food and blisters
our mouths, buries in our meat
its devouring flavor, a carnivore
like us, feeding in darkness and in heat.
May the two of you remain in nightly wedding,
teaching us an equal taste for dark and light,
Salt spraying white upon our meal like day,
Pepper grinding black its accompanying night.

VOCATION

I was fluent in you as in any French,
eased to your syntax and your parts of speech,
as if you were the language I was bred to speak.
It seemed I knew by heart
your long poems and your prayers,
once they leapt to me like fish,
the sea's silver nerves;
you left my tongue drumming them
in funeral meters,
and I collapsed among my native words,
ran my voice counter to its part.
I once kept better quiet,
so braced to your idiom that
silence was apprenticeship, and potent;
my mouth crammed like a gold vault with your name.

A DIALECT OF PARMA

One of them is ham. The other, the one
we are about to hear and practice, spun
on the tape of tongue, is cheese, and you will notice
if you are, say, speaking rice, a vocabulary
of savory unfamiliarity, quite unlike the cool
and juicy ironies common to those reared
to converse in cucumber, proverbs also
almost utterly unknown to students trained
in the wild mushroom argot of the Muscovites,
and incomprehensible to most Americans, those
legendary children of King Midas, whose motto too
was *E pluribus unum*, radiant precursor of a nation
where touch and food and speech are translated quickly
into media, impenetrable, frozen, and synthetic.

There's vitality in poetry written in fluent Parmesan,
whose structures are sometimes circular, heavy salty wheels,
frustrating and obdurate as sweaty work, but capable
of surprising variation, such as one sees in the lusty,
abandoned, golden graffiti, melting like first love,
scribbled on fleshy tortellini.
Consider the thin wafers of its phrases, discrete as flakes of paint
which suggest magnificent architectures, now sublimely
   decomposing.
Surely it evokes epic amalgams of godlike stature, fragile mortality,
when tablespoons float, momentary, sunny, fertile islands,
then vanish forever, Atlantises, into bubbling depths of minestrone.
O rakish Parmesan, coupled with so many dishes, promiscuous and
   human,
Parmesan, core of every dish you flavor, like the heart of man,
image of abundance we would not refuse
even to those we sincerely despise,
,small and galactic as poetry, common and eccentric,
the making of you magnifies, like the telescope of metaphor,
self,

and the great space where self is placed,
so on certain nights of alfresco meals,
we look through what we taste
to delicious, finely grated stars,
strewn generously over blue-glazed skies.

MOVIE MONOSYLLABLES

A man, a woman, an African moon.
The drums, the palms, the dictator.
A revolution in their embrace.
A man, a woman. Coming soon,

A man, a woman. One saw the crime.
An airplane ticket, a star-studded beach;
Doomed, imperial, collapsing waves.
A man, a woman. For the first time,

Locked together in the camera's iris,
a dark-haired stranger, a local wife
cling in closed circuits of a kiss—
Forbidden romance. Larger than life,

A girl, a soldier, a piano score.
One hour till dawn on his last leave
in a world blazing with war and war and war,
A man and a woman. As never before.

SERENADE (AFTER VERLAINE)

A corpse's aria from the tomb—
You can hear my song slice through the noise of dying,
don't you, darling, in your peaceful living room,
recognize my voice, citric and lying?

Open your body, throw open your mind
to the rhythm of this guitar.
For you precisely, I shaped this sound
to sting. Stroke. Scar.

Absolute, I'll sing of the onyx shadow of your eyes,
about your chest where I leapt and fell,
about your hair where I drowned and died
and went to a tangled, curling hell.

A corpse's aria from the tomb—
You can hear my song slice through the noise of dying,
don't you—darling—in your peaceful living room,
recognize my voice, citric and lying?

WEDDING SONG

I.

Earth in her mercy permits us to repeat
the words that fit the only truth we know,
from his hands, between her breasts, all things grow.

Earth in her mercy permits us to repeat
these acts when consecrate couples meet,
the words that fit the only truth we know,
from his hands, between her breasts, all things grow.

Earth in her mercy permits us to repeat
these acts when consecrate couples meet,
and reap from old sentences like harvest wheat,
the words that fit the only truth we know,
from his hands, between her breasts, all things grow.

II.

Listen: a door closes now and tells an end
no one may enter but the married pair,
none challenge holy privacy, or ask a share.

Listen: a door closes now, and tells an end
with fresh soil to till, new fire to tend,
No one may enter but the married pair,
None challenge holy privacy, or ask a share.

Listen: a door closes now, and tells an end
with fresh soil to till, new fire to tend,
neither father, mother, nor beloved friend,
No one may enter but the married pair,
None challenge holy privacy, or ask a share.

III.

So male stars and female end their exile,
and fuse and form in wedding life to life,
that human constellation, man and wife.

So male stars and female end their exile,
accept the union that completes their trial,
and fuse and form in wedding life to life,
that human constellation, man and wife.

So male stars and female end their exile,
begin the crossing of their brilliant mile,
accept the union that completes their trial,
and fuse and form in wedding life to life,
that human constellation, man and wife.

TRANSLATIONS FROM THE AMERICAN

I.

Variety Show

The seasons are changing,
we cannot help it
the leaves cascade onto artificial lawns
and in our parks square as television sets,
spring, autumn, summer flicker in full color,
and wedding, christening, disease goes by,
the restless images of changing channels
on nights that offer no important news
and no network has a good thing on.

II.

Lullaby

Sleep little daughter, sleep while you can,
before your breasts come, and the monthly blood,
while you still lie beneath the general night,
not that darkness condensed into man.

III.

Conundrum

The trouble is there's no word for a man
to whom I've sworn nothing, so can't betray;
nameless, you're neither finite nor immortal;
are you my mistress, then?
Or shall I coldly call you a male interstice?
You or this word. One is unattainable,
and I'll have to choose, as it's language
in the end sustaining what we do,
no hero earns his destiny without his vow.

I'll never find a verb, infertile, but incendiary,
a way of addressing you without endearments,
conjunction to express how utterly—ardently—
I don't love you.

IV.

In an Office

One, two, three;
the champion clock is striking me,
brawny with hours, pins me to the ground,
the clock I punch hits back, the bully.
My skin yellows like a legal pad,
lines ruled evenly across my face,
and the lawyer years write opinions
there of my expensive, unresolved case.

V.

Unrequited Love

I let my silk straps fall, not to charm,
but offer; take me truth, give me that seed
so many contracept; lying, if I must lie, in your arms,
brazen, even desperate, with my need
although I've seen the ones who spent
the night and went disheveled home,
I want you truth; undress with me and breed,
your massive head between my breasts,
my hands ardent on your naked thighs.

So when they come to certify my death
and the coroner scrawls "broken heart," weary-eyed,
and the first wave of photographers arrives,
cameras avid for a full-page spread
to fill the Sunday supplement, let them find me naked,
truth, hair tangled on your pillow, naked,
truth, in your stained, deserted bed.

VI.

Drinking Song

I'm drunk again, I think,
I'm drifting from the kitchen,
doing what I can to navigate,
a balloon aloft on strong tequila.
I use my little will to jettison
the anchoring sandbags of bulky fact,
but somehow at six, I wake on my legs,
with the family supper underway.
The onions are chopped, one finger gashed,
and my heart is cracked like a carton of eggs.

VII.

Ragtime Nocturne

It's two in the morning
and it's too late
The phone doesn't ring
no one cracks an egg

I can't find the light switch
I can't find either leg
it's two in the morning
and it's too late

Absence studies me
cat tensed toward bird
it's two in the morning
and it's too late

What's lost stays missing now
and it's too late
wife wallet word
It's two in the morning

Night lies near my cheek
it's two in the morning
black conch spiraling
and it's too late

I hear a surf of decibel
darkness amplifies, deafening
it's two in the morning
and it's too late.

VIII.

A la Mode

Lady, no one is sufficient master yet
of heart's sad craftsmanship, to forget
your opalescent skin, your drifts of brilliant hair—
we suffer you less in losing than in vigil,
watching you living the same way you began
in your silken time, your white height pliant as a shawl.
But now this raised embroidery of ferns unravels
and the glimmering unbalanced fringe shows tears
and too many years of wrapping any shoulders,
anatomied by any insistent airs,
undone by any fingering hands.

IX.

Child's Play

A child windmilling madly on a bike,
shrilling the soprano-bass motif
of ambulance, the rhythm of emergency,
lurch to the pavement, digitalis,
syringes, bandages, disaster.
Speed—speed is naïve—
he pedals faster.

X.

Love Song

I fall from the hundredth story
                    into love.
Fifty, forty, fifteen floors
                    above,
My kisses plummet toward your eyes,
                    dive
to your shoulders, shatter on your chest.
                    Love
slips deep through your cracked lips;
Fragments which can never be removed.

PERSONAL PRONOUNS

I

(flamenco)

First among the pronouns to stand erect,
I; concentrated might, the Doric column of the alphabet,
spine of sentences, radiating verbs.
How it was in the beginning, I don't forget,
all words then, sworn courtiers, wore my signet.

Foundation of all sounds of pain or lust,
irreducible, raw in flamenco cries'
firelight refrain of wound or coupling, "Ai, ai, ai!"
crucifix of language, I precede knowing: I love, I die.

You

(Jazz improvisations)

I.

Grammar's full-scale costume epic,
universal, there are so many of you;
I've toured the frescoes of your moods,
read the best biographies of you,
watched all night by the shores of you.
My hand is my passport; give me yours,
seal me, grant me asylum in you.

II.

Slum dweller, pond scum; jetsam—
No one asked you, no one wants you.
Squatter, where you live glass shatters,
heads are severed, houses burn,
walls scrawled with obscenities,
and by the thick unconscious breed

the diseased rats of fantasy;
Go back, go back, death ape, guilt-Jew—
I am what I've made of you.

III.

You're my saccharine,
you're my substitute,
my nondairy creamer,
but he's my blood sugar,
he's my blood sugar;
you're my cyclamate.

He's my heat prostration,
he's my hallucination,
he's my steel guillotine,
but you're my sunscreen,
you're my sunscreen,
he's my third-degree burn.

You're my sleeping pill,
you're my aspirin,
my healer, sweet placebo,
and maybe you're my hero,
maybe you're my hero—
he's my heroin.

IV.

Like and unlike's close embrace
formed the bread and wine of you;
there dark finds lucid of its size
as finger slips through shining ring;
you're spliced of sweet and obdurate,
eau-de-vie of strange and intimate,
a chess of vanishing and settlement.
Loved strange and interlocking face—
I don't want to live without you.

He and She

(madrigal)

*for the marriage of Susan Ginsburg
and Peter Nordberg, September 20, 1986*

Montage of anguish and of ecstasy,
mélange of raw blood, of ripe, decanted Burgundy;
in your affections, erratic compatibility,
we trace with awesome clarity
the origins of every reader of these lines, the eros and the agape
that are the cause, if not effect, of human history,
while in the collision or embrace of virility and femininity
glimmer the contours of individual psychology.

In jurisprudence or in poetry,
an insight arrives like that primary
kiss, that answer dancing with inquiry,
the dialectic, dazzling, of a pair of virtuosi,
an interior Rogers and Astaire, a sublime choreography
of sun and moon, night and day, of discovery and fertility,
precious fugue, primal counterpoint and tapestry
of He and She,

parents of tragedy and comedy,
woman and man whose repertory
spans the cantilenas of Callas and Corelli,
and those bonfire dialogues, ardent and witty,
enlacing Katherine Hepburn and Spencer Tracy.
Blessed separate genders, in your union we see
microcosmic creations of ideal societies
reminded that ethics originate in households and sexuality;
we still can hope when hand joins hand so gently
in companionship supremely voluntary,
in cherishing of body and mortal body
to witness a world of sweetness, of symmetry.
Maybe.
Maybe.

It

(Lullaby)

Little it, little eunuch, little culprit,
struck match dropped that burns the house
of the five-year-old who didn't mean to do it.

Little understudy, hid behind curtains, tacit;
all that the tongue-tied point to when
they've lost the name of whatchyamacallit.

Misplaced earring, ticket, stolen loot,
the cache of emeralds the detective found
after the bandit confessed to it.

Half-wit, victim, little scapegoat;
alone and cornered by a crowd of bullies—
"Oh beat it, oh kick it, oh pummel it!"

Focus of tenderness and regret;
peace and quiet and time will heal it,
but it's a pity, oh it's a pity, isn't it?

Little grain, olive pit, conduit
through which the world poured when God saw
that it was good; creation's seed, atom—
and infinite.

PATRICIA STORACE, a native of Mobile, Alabama, was educated at the Madeira School, Barnard College, and the University of Cambridge. Her poetry has appeared in *Parnassus, The Agni Review, Harper's, The Paris Review, The New York Review of Books*, and many other publications. This is her first book.